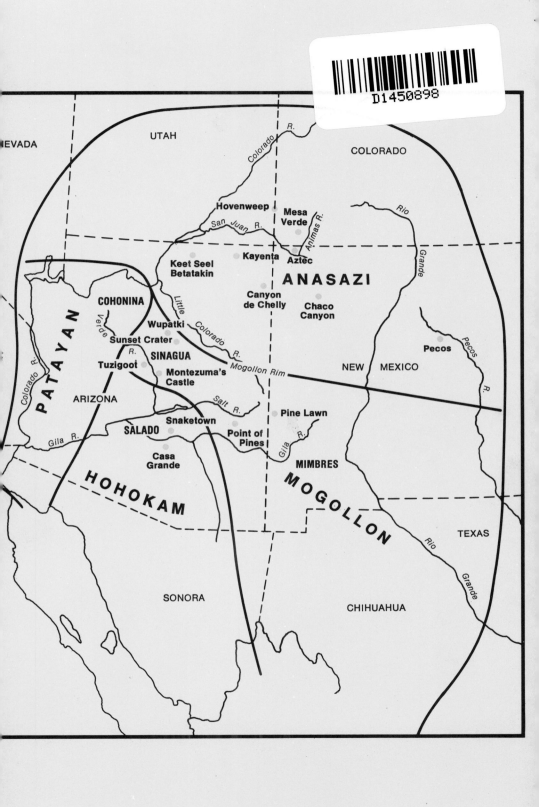

ANCIENT INDIANS
OF THE SOUTHWEST

ANCIENT INDIANS

OF THE

SOUTHWEST

Alfred Tamarin
and
Shirley Glubok

DOUBLEDAY & COMPANY, INC.
GARDEN CITY, NEW YORK

Other Books by Alfred Tamarin

Fire Fighting in America
Japan and the United States: Early Encounters
Voyaging to Cathay—Americans in the China Trade
We Have Not Vanished: Eastern Indians of the United States

Benjamin Franklin: An Autobiographical Portrait
Revolt in Judea: The Road to Masada
The Autobiography of Benvenuto Cellini

Other Books by Shirley Glubok

Art and Archaeology
The Art of Africa
The Art of America from Jackson to Lincoln
The Art of America in the Early Twentieth Century
The Art of America in the Gilded Age
The Art of Ancient Egypt
The Art of Ancient Greece
The Art of Ancient Mexico
The Art of Ancient Peru
The Art of Ancient Rome
The Art of China
The Art of Colonial America
The Art of India
The Art of Japan
The Art of Lands of the Bible
The Art of the Eskimo
The Art of the Etruscans

The Art of the New American Nation
The Art of the North American Indian
The Art of the Old West
The Art of the Northwest Coast Indians
The Art of the Plains Indians
The Art of the South Western Indians
The Art of the Spanish in the United States and Puerto Rico
The Fall of the Aztecs
The Fall of the Incas
Knights in Armor
Dolls Dolls Dolls
Digging in Assyria
Discovering the Royal Tombs at Ur
Discovering Tut-Ankh-Amen's Tomb
Home and Child Life in Colonial Days

Library of Congress Cataloging in Publication Data

Tamarin, Alfred
Ancient Indians of the Southwest
1. Indians of North America—Southwest, New—Antiquities—Juvenile literature.
2. Southwest, New—Antiquities—Juvenile literature.
I. Glubok, Shirley, joint author. II. Title.
E78.S7T28   979'.004'97
ISBN 0-385-09247-4 Trade
0-385-09252-0 Prebound
Library of Congress Catalog Card Number 74–33984

Front cover: Anasazi stone figurine, Museum of New Mexico. Photograph by Alfred Tamarin. Back cover: Canyon de Chelly. Photograph by Alfred Tamarin

5-95

OO.

970.

4

12/20/75

copy # 1

CONTENTS

PICTURE CREDITS AND ACKNOWLEDGMENTS

Endsheet map by Robert Michaels

p. 1: Mimbres bowl, Arizona State Museum, University of Arizona, Photograph by Alfred Tamarin.

p. 11, top: University of Colorado Museum. Photograph by Alfred Tamarin.

p. 11, bottom: Museum of New Mexico. Photograph by Alfred Tamarin.

p. 13: Canyon de Chelly, Arizona. Photograph by Alfred Tamarin.

p. 16, top: Arizona State Museum, University of Arizona. Photograph by Alfred Tamarin.

p. 16, bottom: Arizona State Museum, University of Arizona. Photograph by Alfred Tamarin.

p. 17, top: Arizona State Museum, University of Arizona. Photograph by Alfred Tamarin.

p. 17, bottom: Arizona State Museum, University of Arizona. Photograph by Alfred Tamarin.

p. 18: Denver Museum of Natural History. Photograph by Alfred Tamarin.

p. 19: Museum of New Mexico. Photograph by Alfred Tamarin.

p. 20: Photograph by Alfred Tamarin.

p. 22: Courtesy of University of Colorado Museum.

p. 24: Canyon de Chelly, Arizona. Photograph by Alfred Tamarin.

p. 25: Courtesy of Museum of New Mexico.

p. 26: Museum of New Mexico. Photograph by Alfred Tamarin.

p. 27: University of Colorado Museum. Photograph by Alfred Tamarin.

p. 30: National Museum of Finland, Helsinki.

p. 33: Maxwell Museum of Anthropology, University of New Mexico. Photograph by Alfred Tamarin.

p. 37, top: Museum of New Mexico. Photograph by Alfred Tamarin.

p. 37, bottom: Courtesy of Smithsonian Institution.

p. 38, top: Courtesy of Smithsonian Institution.

p. 38, bottom left: After Awatovi mural, courtesy of Peabody Museum of Archaeology and Ethnology, Harvard University.

p. 38, bottom right: Courtesy of Peabody Museum of Archaeology and Ethnology, Harvard University.

p. 40: University of Colorado Museum. Photograph by Alfred Tamarin.

p. 41, top: Museum of New Mexico. Photograph by Alfred Tamarin.

p. 41, bottom: Museum of New Mexico. Photograph by Alfred Tamarin.

p. 42, top: Museum of New Mexico. Photograph by Alfred Tamarin.

p. 42, bottom: University of Colorado Museum. Photograph by Alfred Tamarin.

p. 45: Arizona State Museum, University of Arizona. Photograph by Helga Teiwes.

p. 48: Maxwell Museum of Anthropology, University of New Mexico. Photograph by Alfred Tamarin.

p. 49: Arizona State Museum, University of Arizona. Photograph by Alfred Tamarin.

p. 50: Arizona State Museum, University of Arizona. Photograph by Alfred Tamarin.

p. 51: Arizona State Museum, University of Arizona. Photograph by Alfred Tamarin.

p. 52: Arizona State Museum, University of Arizona. Photograph by Alfred Tamarin.

p. 53: Arizona State Museum, University of Arizona. Photograph by Alfred Tamarin.

p. 54: Arizona State Museum, University of Arizona. Photograph by Alfred Tamarin.

p. 58: Wupatki National Monument, U. S. Department of the Interior, National Park Service. Photograph by George A. Grant.

p. 59: Wupatki National Monument. Photograph by Alfred Tamarin.

p. 60: Tuzigoot National Monument, U. S. Department of the Interior, National Park Service. Photograph by George A. Grant.

p. 61: Photograph by Alfred Tamarin.

p. 62: Smithsonian Institution, National Anthropological Archives.

p. 63: Arizona State Museum, University of Arizona. Photograph by Alfred Tamarin.

p. 65: San Diego Museum of Man. Photograph by Alfred Tamarin.

p. 68: Courtesy of University of Colorado Museum.

p. 69: Museum of New Mexico. Photograph by Alfred Tamarin.

p. 72: Museum of New Mexico. Photograph by Alfred Tamarin.

p. 73, top: Courtesy of Mesa Verde National Park, Howard Short Collection. Photograph by Alfred Tamarin.

p. 73, bottom: University of Colorado Museum. Photograph by Alfred Tamarin.

p. 74, top: Courtesy of Mesa Verde National Park. Photograph by Alfred Tamarin.

p. 74, bottom: University of Colorado Museum. Photograph by Alfred Tamarin.

p. 75: University of Colorado Museum. Photograph by Alfred Tamarin.

p. 76: Courtesy of Mesa Verde National Park. Photograph by Alfred Tamarin.

p. 77, top: Museum of New Mexico. Photograph by Alfred Tamarin.

p. 77, bottom: Courtesy of Mesa Verde National Park. Photograph by Alfred Tamarin.

p. 78: University of Colorado Museum. Photograph by Alfred Tamarin.

p. 79: Courtesy of Mesa Verde National Park. Photograph by Alfred Tamarin.

p. 80: University of Colorado Museum. Photograph by Alfred Tamarin.
p. 81: Courtesy of Mesa Verde National Park. Photograph by Alfred Tamarin.
p. 84: Aztec National Monument. Photograph by Alfred Tamarin.
p. 85: Courtesy Superintendent, Chaco National Monument.
p. 86–87: Canyon de Chelly, U. S. Department of the Interior, National Park Service. Photograph by George A. Grant.
p. 88: Navajo National Monument, U. S. Department of the Interior, National Park Service. Photograph by Fred E. Mang, Jr.
p. 91: Navajo National Monument, U. S. Department of the Interior, National Park Service. Photograph by Fred E. Mang, Jr.
p. 92: Courtesy of Mesa Verde National Park. Photograph by Alfred Tamarin.

The authors gratefully acknowledge the kind assistance of:
J. Richard Ambler, Associate Professor of Anthropology, Northern Arizona University; Sally Black, Administrative Assistant, Maxwell Museum of Anthropology, University of New Mexico; A. Lynn Coffin, Fort Collins, Colorado; Richard Conn, Curator of Native Arts, Denver Art Museum; Charles C. Di Peso, Director, Amerind Foundation, Dragoon, Arizona; Alfred E. Dittert, Professor of Anthropology, Arizona State University, Tempe; Florence Ellis, Albuquerque, New Mexico; Ernie Escalante, Tuzigoot National Monument, Arizona; Robert C. Euler; George Ewing, Director, Museum of New Mexico, Santa Fe; Nancy Fox, Curator of Anthropology Collections, Museum of New Mexico; Emil W. Haury, Fred A. Riecker Distinguished Professor of Anthropology, University of Arizona, and Chairman, Advisory Board of National Parks, Historic Sites, Buildings, and Monuments; Ken Hedges, Associate Curator, San Diego Museum of Man; Ernest Leavitt, Curator of Exhibits, Arizona State Museum, University of Arizona; Alexander J. Lindsay, Jr., Curator of Anthropology, Museum of Northern Arizona, Flagstaff; Robert H. Lister, Chaco Center, National Park Service, Albuquerque; Stewart L. Peckham, Curator-in-charge, Anthropology Division, Museum of New Mexico; Albert H. Schroeder, Interpretive Specialist, National Park Service, Southwest Region, Santa Fe; Gilbert R. Wenger, Chief Park Archaeologist, Mesa Verde National Park, Colorado; H. M. Wormington, Adjunct Professor of Anthropology, Colorado College, and Research Associate in Paleo-Indian Studies, University of Colorado Museum;
and especially: Raymond H. Thompson, Director, Arizona State Museum, University of Arizona, and Joe Ben Wheat, Curator, University of Colorado Museum, Boulder.

THE ANCIENT PEOPLE

THE BIG-GAME HUNTERS

The little band of ancient hunters crept along cautiously, stopping often to listen for the sounds of the game lumbering through the underbrush ahead. An icy wind swept down from the slowly melting glacier, but the sun was warmer than it had been for a long time. The hunters moved on, carrying sharp, pointed stone spears to bring down the fleeing mammoth—or was it a mastodon? The elephantlike mammal pushed forward blindly, trying to escape its pursuers.

The hunters themselves did not realize that every step was taking them farther and farther east into a land where no human being had ever walked before. The men did not know that, pursuing their prey, they were stepping off a broad land bridge that then connected Asia with what is now Alaska. The hunting band was composed of the first humans to set foot on the continent of North America.

Long ago, North and South America abounded with large animal life. Big beasts roamed the land. A huge woolly humpbacked mammoth with long tusks that curved inward stood taller than the modern elephant. Almost as huge was the mastodon, with sweeping tusks that spread six feet from tip to tip. Herds of gigantic bison galloped over the grassy plains. The ground sloth padded along on the sides of its enormous paws. Beavers were the size of modern-day bears, and bears were larger than the largest of today's grizzlies. Ten species of primitive horses ranged the forests and plains. Ancient camels stood taller than the varieties that exist today. The American continents still teemed with animals—lions and wildcats, saber-toothed tigers, wolves, musk oxen, caribou, and other species, many of which became extinct thousands of years ago.

The human animal, however, did not evolve, or develop, in either North or South America. When human hunters finally crossed over from Asia to Alaska, they were already fully developed. Archaeologists today are discovering more and more about the earliest inhabitants in the Americas by studying their bones and skulls found in ancient burials, the stone weapons and utensils that they once used, and the remains of the dwellings they lived in long ago. Their studies lead the archaeologists to believe that the first Indian hunters were Asians, because old skeletons found in both America and Siberia prove to be of similar physical types. Along with the skeletal remains, stone tools have been found on both continents which are also similar.

No one knows for certain exactly how long ago the first men and women came to America. Stones, bits of bone, and fire-hardened wood, which may have been very primitive tools, have been found, suggesting that people were in parts of America as long ago as 35,000 years or even more. Because no spearheads or projectile points were found with these primitive tools, this very early period is sometimes referred to as a "pre-projectile point horizon." Definite evidence, however, proves that people had certainly come at least 13,000 years ago.

By that time the hunters who were filtering into the Americas from Asia had acquired many useful skills. The men hunted in bands, for only as a group could they successfully attack the mammoth beasts. They knew how to make hunting weapons by shaping stones into powerful and deadly spearheads, which could bring down animals much larger than a human. They were already able to fashion stone knives and scrapers to cut meat and clean animal hides, which they used as clothing. The ancient hunters could make projectile points of bone to use against smaller game. They also used mortars and pestles made of stone to grind the nuts and seeds that they gathered for food.

The first Indian men and women probably knew how to weave baskets, mats, nets, bags, and even shoes. They had learned how to make fire, for both cooking and warmth. In all probability they were accompanied into America by dogs that had been domesticated in Asia.

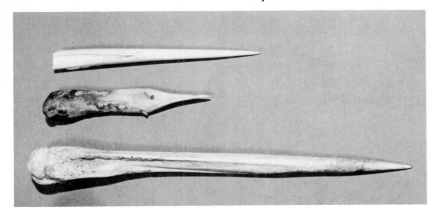

BONE AWLS

The newcomers to America may already have been organized into family groups, and they seem to have brought with them a system of beliefs in gods and spirits. One of the ceremonial objects they carried is still in use today, fifteen thousand years later, by native people in California. A wooden, paddlelike wand, called a bull-roarer, produced a roaring noise when it was whirled rapidly through the air.

BULL-ROARER

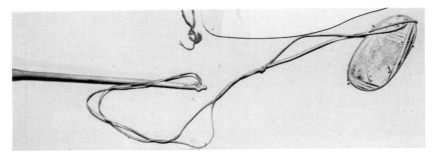

When the first hunters reached North America, the bridge of land linking Siberia to the American continent stretched across a thousand miles at its widest point. The area, which is now covered by the waters of the Bering Sea and Bering Strait, is referred to as Beringia.

During the thousands of years known as the Ice Age, Beringia was above water on several different occasions. During these periods the earth's surface was covered with blankets of ice and snow, often miles thick. Sometimes, however, the temperature would rise, and the snow and ice would melt. Water would pour back into the sea, and the surface of the oceans would rise, covering huge areas of land. During these times Beringia would be under water, often 150 feet deep.

When the temperature fell again, water evaporating from the ocean became snow and would fall on the frozen land, piling higher and higher without melting. More and more water from the sea evaporated, but little flowed back to make up the loss. As a result, the level of the ocean surface dropped lower and lower during these times until the land bridge, Beringia, reappeared.

Toward the end of the Ice Age, while Beringia was dry land, the Wisconsin glacier, an ice blanket that covered the northern part of North America, started to melt. Pathways began to open in the ice, and stretches of earth appeared, in which plants could take root and sprout. The green growth, which made it possible for grazing animals to sustain themselves, lured on the mammoth or mastodon, escaping from the pursuing hunters. The huntsmen pressed on after their prey. The peopling of America had begun.

Once in America the early hunters continued trailing the game. Slowly, the little band of men and women pushed inland and southward, to be followed soon thereafter by other hunting parties in pursuit of other game. The trickle of people continued over the centuries as long as the Beringia land bridge was above water. On the North American continent the game trails led down pathways that had opened up in the ice and wandered off to the eastern slopes of the mountains and into great, grassy plains. The hunting bands followed slowly but steadily. Other game drew the hunters along other routes, some of which followed the valleys along the Pacific Coast and reached into warm, dry flatlands. For several thousand years the hunters spread out

HUNTER WITH BOW AND ARROW: ROCK PAINTING

across the continent, going wherever the big beasts led them. In areas that are now desert, wild plants, nuts, and berries were gathered to add to the hunter's usual diet of meat. In time, the descendants of the early Asian hunters reached the southernmost tip of South America, nine thousand miles away from the land bridge between Asia and Alaska.

Migrations from Asia had been occurring for just a few centuries when the climate changed again. The weather grew warmer, and the snows started to melt. Water once again flowed back into the sea, raising the level of the ocean's surface until Beringia was under water. But a link had been forged between Asia and America that would never again be broken. Now, people traveled between the two continents by boat across the Bering Sea, which separates them today. New ideas and the development of new tools and skills in Asia sooner or later spread to America. During the course of thousands of years the polished stone adze was brought across, followed by spoons, combs of bone or antler horn, and toggle harpoons for spearing fish. And sometime during these early years a new hunting weapon was developed in Asia and crossed over to America—the bow and arrow.

Asiatic people continued migrating to North America. The Eskimos paddled their kayaks from one shore to another. Eskimos still live today on both sides of the Bering Strait. A later wave of immigrants from Asia were the Athapascans, who made their way slowly inland, reaching areas where their descendants live to this day. Some Athapascans eventually arrived in the dry desert lands of what is now the Southwest United States. They remained there to become the forebears of the modern Apache and Navajo.

The early Indian newcomers from Asia found the weather in America much colder and wetter than it is today. The topography, or surface, of the land was also different. Dense vegetation flourished in areas that are now deserts. There were wide grassy plains, dotted with swamps and lakes, some ten times larger than their present size.

The thick grasses supported a varied animal life. The native ancestor of the horse grazed alongside ancient animal species now extinct—the four-pronged antelope, a gigantic shaggy-maned bison, and a huge camel. An enormous wolf preyed on the ground sloth, the deer, and the piglike peccary. Some of the megafauna—the giant beasts—such as the mammoth and the mastodon, stood as high as thirteen feet at the shoulder. The mammoth and mastodon are both ancient species of the elephant. For this reason the early Indians who pursued them have been called the Elephant Hunters.

The Elephant Hunters begin what some scholars call the Big-Game Hunter tradition in America. In archaeological terms the Elephant Hunters marked the dawn of the Ancient, or Paleo-Indian, tradition, which spanned an era of more than five thousand years.

Herds of mammoths and mastodons wandered all over the lush grasslands of the North American continent from the Pacific to the Atlantic Ocean, stalked everywhere by the Elephant Hunters. East of the Rocky Mountains the elephant-hunting Indians have been given the name Clovis man, so called because their spearheads were first discovered on a high plain near the town of Clovis, New Mexico. The area is now arid and wind-swept, but thousands of years ago it was covered by glacial lakes and ponds.

In a location near Clovis known as Blackwater Draw No. 1, the bones of a mammoth were found along with two spear points. The spearheads were large and grooved, or fluted, partly up the length of the point. A flute in a projectile point is made by removing a single flake from the stone. The sides and edges were formed by a process of flaking or chipping with a stone tool. The weapons were given the name Clovis points. Later excavations at Blackwater revealed other stone tools, such as scrapers and hammerstones, as well as cylinders of bone, which might have been used as spear tips.

Clovis points are spearheads designed especially for hunting large animals. The points are too heavy and too big to be used as arrow tips. Clovis spearheads, bound by thongs of sinew to a wooden shaft, were used as thrusting or sticking weapons, like bayonets. The spears were probably not hurled or thrown. The hunters stalked their elephantlike prey, prodding the big beasts with spears until the animals were driven into a shallow lake or swamp where they became helplessly mired in the mud.

The Blackwater Draw site at Clovis was not only a hunting ground but probably also a camp. Its use by the Elephant Hunters was revealed by the Clovis points which were dug up at the deepest level of an archaeological excavation, or dig, and dated around 9000 B.C. The hunting at Clovis continued for several thousand years.

Clovis projectile points, lying close to bones of mammoths, were unearthed by archaeologists near the town of Naco, on the border of Arizona and the Mexican state of Sonora. The mammoths had probably been hunted down with these spear points. One is made of chert, a flintlike rock.

The bones of nine young mammoths were found, along with the skeletal remains of other animals, in an archaeological site at Lehner, near the town of Hereford, Arizona. Near the jawbone of an ancient bison, known as *bison antiquus,* a spearhead was dug up. It was made of a stone called chalcedony, a variety of quartz.

Over the centuries, as the weather changed and the grasslands

CLOVIS STONE TOOL: SCRAPER FROM MURRAY SPRINGS, ARIZONA

BONE WRENCH FROM MURRAY SPRINGS, ARIZONA

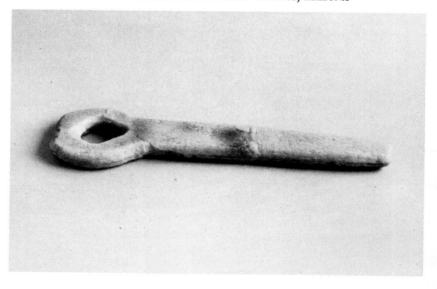

CLOVIS PROJECTILE POINT FROM NACO, ARIZONA

CLOVIS PROJECTILE POINT FROM LEHNER, ARIZONA

FOLSOM PROJECTILE POINT

dried up, the giant mammoths and mastodons, which fed on vegetation, became extinct. Several species of giant bison also died out. The era of the Elephant Hunters had come to an end.

Instead, a new type of Indian hunter evolved, using new kinds of spear points designed for smaller game. These hunters pursued the American bison, which has been mistakenly called the buffalo; they have therefore become known as the Buffalo Hunters. They ran after their prey, which roamed over the plains east of the Rocky Mountains.

The Buffalo Hunters are also known by the name Folsom men, after a town in northeastern New Mexico where a new type of projectile point was found, together with the bones of thirty bison. The bones of the bison and the new variety of spearheads were discovered in the dried-up remains of what had once been a marsh or watering hole where the animals came to drink or to wallow in the mud. The different shape of the spearheads revealed the changes that had taken place in the lives and hunting habits of the Indians.

The new kind of spearhead is called a Folsom point. It was probably adapted from the earlier Clovis point, but it was smaller and more delicately made. It was widest at its midsection rather than at its base, which was cut in a concave curve and had tiny, earlike projections at each end. Most noticeable were the flutes, or channels, that marked almost the entire face of both sides. Folsom points were considered most effective against the bison, which had become the chief game for the new Indian hunters.

A Folsom point was found lying near the skull of a giant *bison antiquus*, which it had probably killed. The animal lived about ten thousand years ago.

Besides being buffalo hunters, Folsom Indians supplemented their meat diets with wild plants and fruits. While they roamed the plains following the game, they probably gathered seeds and roots when they could find them. But Folsom man was not ranging over as much of the continent as the Clovis hunters had before him. His hunting ground was narrowing, even though it still covered vast areas of mountains and plains. Folsom points have been discovered in eastern New Mexico, Texas, Colorado, Wyoming, and Montana.

SKULL OF ANCIENT BISON, WITH FOLSOM PROJECTILE POINT, AT RIGHT

In northern Colorado near the Wyoming border, Folsom-type spear points were found in a dry gulch, which is known as the Lindenmeier site. The spot is thought to have been a hunting ground and a campground for Folsom hunters. In addition to the characteristic fluted spear points, the site produced chipped-stone knives, choppers, and scrapers, as well as other weapons and tools needed by people who depended on hunting for food and animal skins. The Lindenmeier site was occupied around 8800 B.C., about the time that the Wisconsin glacier was retreating and the weather started warming up again. The bones of extinct bison were found in the Lindenmeier site, but no traces of the mammoth.

Another type of early projectile point has been unearthed in a cave in the Sandia Mountains near Albuquerque, New Mexico.

During the thousands of years when the Big-Game Hunters roamed first the entire continent and then the Great Plains, the weather in North America changed. The warm weather began to cool until, around 5000 B.C., the temperate climate that is known today set in.

The Paleo-Indian tradition, as a whole, was coming to its end. When big game became extinct, the hunters turned to the smaller animals for their prey. The last of the ancient hunting traditions is called the Plano Complex. During this stage many new types of projectile points were produced in the High Plains. They were lanceolate, or lance-shaped, in form, slender, long, and large, made by pressure flaking—a process of shaping a projectile point by pressing off flakes of stone with a pointed stick or bone. They may have developed from the earlier fluted Clovis and Folsom forms. Two main groupings have been distinguished within the Plano. One, called Plainview, consists of unfluted points, resembling the Clovis and Folsom fluted types. Included in this group are the Plainview, Midland, Milnesand, and Meserve forms. The second group is known as Parallel-flaked and comprises such types as the Scottsbluff, Eden, Cody, Olsen-Chubbock, and Agate Basin points.

OLSEN-CHUBBOCK POINTS

But small game does not range over an entire continent like giant elephants and bison. The smaller animals lived in more limited areas. The hunters, too, found it unnecessary to roam quite so far.

THE HUNTER-GATHERERS

Indian hunters, pursuing big game, had for centuries trailed their prey into the grassy plains between the Cascade Mountains of southern Oregon and the Rocky Mountain ranges in Idaho. For thousands of years the vast grasslands, supporting a varied animal life, had also covered most of Nevada, western Utah, and an eastern section of California. But changing weather turned the green savannas into semiarid deserts. Large lakes dried up, some shrinking to fractions of their former size, some evaporating completely.

The territory that includes parts of six states is now known as the Great Basin, because all of its streams flow inward to lakes, like the Great Salt Lake, or disappear into the sands of the desert without ever reaching the sea.

The change of pasture and climate drove herds of big animals over the mountains to the plains where the grazing lands were richer and where water was more plentiful. The smaller animals retreated to the mountains, emptying the lowlands of much of its game. Hunting for food became increasingly difficult, and a substitute for meat became necessary. The desert hunters were faced with the need of finding new food if they hoped to survive. The people became gatherers, collecting seeds, berries, and edible roots to sustain themselves.

In the course of time, around 7000 B.C., while the Big-Game Hunters were dying out, the hunters and gatherers from the Great Basin found their way into the mountains and tablelands of the Southwest, which includes parts of Colorado and Utah, all of Arizona and New Mexico, and sections of the Mexican states of Sonora and Chihuahua. The Southwest is vast and varied. It comprises plateau country—mountain tablelands or mesas, a mile

MOUNTAIN GOATS: ROCK PAINTING

or more high, cut by hundreds of canyons with sheer cliffs or rocky talus slopes. Parallel ranges of mountains, divided by basins, run across the international border, and river valleys cut through hot, dry desert lands.

Running through the southwestern area like a giant spinal column is the Continental Divide, the line of mountain ranges and peaks that determines the directions in which the rivers drain to the sea. Flowing eastward from the Divide toward the Gulf of Mexico and the Atlantic Ocean are the Rio Grande, all of its tributaries, the Pecos River, and the Mimbres, which buries itself in the earth. The western-flowing rivers, draining toward the Gulf of California and the Pacific Ocean, are the Colorado River, the Little Colorado and all of the subsidiary branches, the San Juan, the Salt, and the upper and lower Gila.

The hunter-gatherers, who wandered into the Southwest, moved in small bands. A band might consist of an extended family —a man and a woman, their children, and their grandchildren. The pattern of life was somewhat nomadic, but the wandering was not aimless. The groups moved regularly from one place to another—a river valley, a mountain slope, an upland area—returning year after year for the seasonal reappearance of animals or plants. Hundreds of years of experience had led the people to know what kinds of food they could find.

The wandering bands traveled with few possessions, but they always carried two objects that were characteristic of their new way of life: a basket and a milling stone. The baskets were necessary to gather the plant food that had come to make up most of the new diet. The milling stones were used to grind the roots, berries, and seeds into a flour or paste.

What the early wanderers gathered and ate can be surmised from the vegetable food of the Paiute Indians, who still live in the Southwest. As recently as a century ago the diet of this late hunting-and-gathering people included acorns, piñon nuts, various grass seeds, cress, sunflowers, sego, lily bulbs, bulrushes, berries, and assorted roots. These plants and roots were ground on a milling stone and then cooked into a mush or gruel. To be edible, seeds were usually parched in a flat basket by being mixed with live coals and constantly shaken to keep the coals from scorching the seeds or burning the basket.

Meat was obtained by hunting the desert animals with snares and nets, throwing sticks, darts, and spears. Meat was often

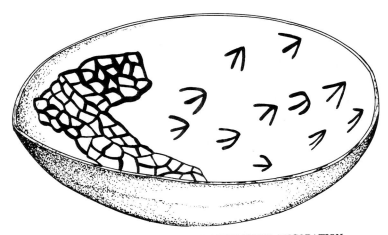

SNARE FOR NETTING BIRDS, POTTERY BOWL DECORATION

HUNTER WITH BIRDS, MIMBRES BOWL DECORATION

prepared by roasting, and any surplus was dried, pounded into a powder, and preserved in a bag.

Foraging for plant foods and hunting small game kept the desert wanderers alive after the big game and the Big-Game Hunters had disappeared. The hunter-gatherer tradition that found its place in the southwestern desert never vanished. It has persisted into modern times among the Pueblo Indians of the Rio Grande Valley, the Acoma, Isleta, Hopi, and Zuñi tribes of New Mexico and Arizona. The Yuman tribes of the lower Colorado River Valley are descendants of the ancient hunting-gathering people, as are the Indians of southern Arizona, who still live in hot, semiarid deserts.

One branch of the ancient desert people, who, centuries be-

RABBIT, MIMBRES BOWL DECORATION

fore, had left the Great Basin to wander in the Southwest, has been given a name in modern times: Cochise. The name comes from Cochise County, Arizona, where traces of the early wandering people were first found. The emergence of the Cochise is dated around 5000 B.C.

For thousands of years the Cochise wandered over the mountains and through the valleys, living in caves along the courses of streams and near the mud-caked, flat, dry beds of ancient lakes, called playas. Meat was scarce, an occasional rabbit supplying most of the edible game available. Plant foods were usually plentiful, but droughts or extremes of heat or cold could ruin the supply. Famines were not uncommon.

Sometime during the thousand-year span between 3000 B.C.

and 2000 B.C., a very primitive type of corn, or maize, was brought up into the Southwest from Mexico, where it had been cultivated for thousands of years. The pollen of wild maize in Mexico has been dated as far back as 80,000 B.C. Later varieties of primitive maize were pod corn and flint corn. Pod corn, in a wild or very early state of domestication, has proved to be as old as the fifth millennium B.C. Like popcorn, the kernels of pod corn are each separately enclosed. Flint corn is a hard, horny, tropical variety, with short, flat kernels.

The Cochise in the Southwest were ready to receive early corn from Mexico and to plant and cultivate it. The ancient Indian seed gatherers were able to grow the corn not only because their soil was adequate and the growing season satisfactory, but also because they had the necessary skills and tools. They could already weave baskets in which to store corn, and for countless years they had been using stone grinding tools to pulverize seeds and nuts. Now the milling stones could also be used to prepare corn pastes and gruels for food.

Stone pestles are still used for grinding foods in the Southwest. Modern implements, the mano and the metate, derive from the ancient milling tools. The metate is a large stone with a hollowed-out trough in which seeds or kernels are placed to be ground into a pulpy paste when the mano is pushed over them. The word "mano" is Spanish, meaning "hand." "Metate" is a combined word, deriving from both Spanish and the Indian language of the Aztecs of Mexico.

The early, primitive forms of maize have been found in southwestern caves, all within a radius of one hundred miles of one another. In Bat Cave in the Pine Lawn region of west-central New Mexico the earliest seedlings of corn north of Mexico were found and estimated to be four to five thousand years old. Archaeologists discovered additional evidence of primitive corn in the Tularosa and Cordova caves nearby. Deposits of maize pollen were also discovered in the soil of the Point of Pines region in eastern Arizona. All of the finds of early corn in the Southwest were in terrain very much like the areas in Mexico where the corn originated. The cave finds were all in wooded upland valleys, six thousand feet or more high.

Over the years the primitive corn passed from Indian band to Indian band, moving slowly along the mountainsides and up the river valleys from Mexico into the Southwest. Some southwestern areas were not suited for corn cultivation, but here and there, river valleys opened up into rich flatlands, ideal for planting. The Cochise set their few kernels of corn seed in the ground and wandered off to continue the search for edible berries and roots. In time these Indians came back to look after their plants and to harvest a few ears.

Centuries ago, primitive corn varieties provided extra nourishment for the wandering Cochise. It was a welcome supplement to their uncertain diet. About the same time that the corn was being diffused from Mexico, an early variety of squash was brought under cultivation in the Southwest, often in the same plots as the corn. The tiny gardens of corn and squash narrowed the range of the Cochise's wandering. The Indians found themselves confined to a mountainside, a high plain, or a river valley, where small game animals could be trapped and wild plants and berries gathered.

The Cochise were still hunters and gatherers, but with the introduction of a fairly dependable corn plant that could be cultivated and harvested, they began to settle down.

Around 1000 B.C. a new, more vigorous strain of corn reached the Southwest from Mexico. The improved maize variety could be cultivated more easily than the older types; its yield was more reliable. Along with it, another new plant was introduced, the red kidney bean.

The Indians needed more permanent homesites, close to their patches of growing corn. Often they set up shelters in caves in the sides of a cliff near their cornfields. They had to have better milling stones, which they developed. They dug pits in the ground to serve as storage bins for the corn. The larger storage pits were sometimes used as shelters by the Indians, becoming the simplest form of semi-underground or pithouse. Late in the period of the Cochise these pithouses were grouped together to form villagelike settlements. And as agricultural activities increased, the first forms of pottery were made, and soon afterward baked-clay figurines of people and animals.

The story of the early Indians in the Southwest has been revealed by archaeological finds in Ventana Cave, 110 miles from Tucson, Arizona. Inside the cave archaeologists found piles

of refuse—remains of pottery, projectile points, and basketry—
which had been discarded by the ancient people. The trash, protected from erosion by the action of sun, wind, and rain, had sur-
vived for centuries. By studying the layers of trash, archaeologists were able to fix the dates of the various settlements that had
been made inside the rock shelter. Since the refuse in the topmost
layer would have been discarded by the most recent inhabitants,
the more deeply the material was buried in the trash heap,
the older it could be assumed to be.

The piles of refuse in Ventana Cave disclosed a history of
Southwest people over a period of ten thousand years. At the
very bottom of the pile were two projectile points: an unfluted
Folsom and a truncated, or cut-off, leaf-shaped point with notches
at the corners. Also found were the bones of an extinct horse and
a sloth. The earliest occupants of the cave had been simple hunters. A higher layer in the cave revealed the presence of desert
wild plant gatherers. The topmost remains—and therefore the
most recent—provided evidence of corn and corn cultivation. The
last inhabitants of Ventana Cave had become farmers.

The transition of the hunting-gathering Cochise into farmers
was made clear in even fuller detail in Tularosa and Cordova
caves. Protected by the dry atmosphere inside the caves, many

STONE AX

examples of late Cochise culture were found fully preserved. Excavation revealed maize, beans, squash, gourds, and a wide variety of wild plants such as cacti, yucca pods, acorns, walnuts, grass, and sunflower seeds, all of which were discovered in both a lower pre-pottery level and a higher stratum, in which the first signs of pottery came to light. Other articles were preserved in both the late Cochise stage and the farming level which followed. These included sandals, cradles, nets, carrying bags, coiled baskets, twined baskets, leather bags, reed flutes, wooden dice, spear-throwers, and darts. There was a piece of unfired pottery inside a basket. Other finds included chipped-stone projectile points, stone knives, scrapers, choppers, grinding tools, manos, metates, hammers, tools and ornaments of bone, and beads and bracelets made of shell. The Cochise hunter-gatherers had entered a new stage.

THE MOGOLLON

THE MEN OF THE MOUNTAINS

A range of mountains in central Arizona extends south and east into New Mexico, forming the edge of an expanse of high plateau country that stretches off to the horizon. The mountain formation has been named the Mogollon Rim, after a Spanish official who lived in the early eighteenth century. Other mountains nearby run north and south in parallel ranges, extending down to the Mexican border and beyond.

The mountains in New Mexico and in the bordering Mexican states of Chihuahua and Sonora reach considerable heights, and the rain clouds dump ample moisture on the hillsides. Near the mountain peaks are Douglas fir trees and aspen, which quiver in the wind. At lower elevations the forests become piñon, juniper, and pine. Still farther down the slopes are stands of oak and growths of chaparral, which merge into grasslands.

From the Mogollon Rim the terrain southward loses elevation, dropping several thousand feet into the valleys of the southern basin, where the rainfall is more meager. The hotter valleys are covered with desert grasses, mesquite, and cactus.

The early Indians of this varied countryside have been given the same name as the mountain rim—Mogollon. The Mogollon farmers succeeded the hunting-and-gathering Cochise, who had been in the Southwest for centuries.

The earliest of the Mogollon farming traditions began around 100 B.C., two centuries after an improved corn variety had reached the Southwest from Mexico. The new corn, a marked advance over the early primitive corn which had been grown for

WOMAN WITH DIGGING STICK, MIMBRES BOWL DECORATION

several thousand years, hastened the beginning of farming and the start of building fixed homes near the cornfields and water supplies. The advent of a primitive village life, pithouse architecture, and pottery established the Mogollon's initial phase.

Mogollon corn farmers continued to live in southwestern New Mexico, central Arizona, and the Mexican states of Chihuahua and Sonora for fifteen hundred years. Over the centuries their skills as farmers improved. They introduced new crops and turned old tools to new and different purposes. The pointed sticks, for instance, which had once been used to dig out roots and tubers, were made to hollow out storage pits for corn and house pits for shelter. If the digging stick had a crook at one end, it could be made to pull out small game from burrows in the earth.

The digging stick could also be used for planting seeds in the little hills of earth that the Indian farmer piled up. Into holes poked with his long pointed stick the Mogollon planter could set the new corn seeds.

Maize, squash, and beans, all of which were being grown by Mogollon farmers, required care and cultivation if the crops were to flourish. The Mogollon people began to build permanent houses near their fields, choosing community sites on a high ridge or secluded bluff on a nearby mountainside. The pithouse villages were relatively small, averaging about twenty houses in each. There were also hamlets consisting of only two or three houses, and even individual units were built in isolated spots.

The early Mogollon seemed to have an urge to live in comparative seclusion for reasons that are not certain. They may have needed the protection of high ground from foreign marauders, though no signs of man-made fortifications have been found. The higher locations afforded better drainage and perhaps cooler breezes in the hotter temperatures. Some archaeologists have even suggested that the Indians had the simple wish to have a good outlook over the mountain countryside.

Certainly, however, the shortage of arable soil in the valleys made every inch of good farm land essential for crop cultivation rather than house building.

A Mogollon house was a semi-subterranean pithouse, which seems to have been an ancient concept in North America, derived from Asia, but no one knows when or how. The Mogollon house builder dug a shallow excavation in the ground and in it erected a house, half above and half below the surface. The early Mogollon pithouses were rounded. The sides of the pit formed the lower sidings of the dwelling. The upper walls consisted of a framework of logs set upright. At first these logs also supported roof timbers, called vigas, which were covered with brush and twigs and plastered with earth and stones. Later, the conical roof was erected, with a large center pole inside the house for the main support. A flat roof could be laid on four posts, set in each corner.

Inside his semi-underground dwelling the early Mogollon Indian dug a fire pit and a storage pit. The storage pit had straight sides and was not lined. Outside the structure there might be another storage pit, usually bell-shaped.

Early Mogollon pithouses were entered directly by a ramp leading down from the ground level. There was a very short antechamber or none at all. Eventually in the northern regions of Mogollon country an entryway was added to the pithouse, which could also be used as a sort of storage room. This entrance area has been called a "front porch" room. After a while the "front porch" area was transformed into a ventilator shaft to provide an escape for the smoke of the fire that was usually burning inside.

An important feature of Mogollon architecture was the large ceremonial house, known as the great kiva. These pithouse structures were usually three or more times larger than the usual dwelling. The shapes of the early kivas varied. Some were round, some shaped like a D, others like beans. Most contained fire pits and excavations in the floor, resembling the storage pits. Mogollon villages clustered around the great kivas, which were the center of the people's religious life.

An attempt to reconstruct the social life of the Mogollon Indians has been made by studying the present-day societies of the Hopi and Zuñi Indians, who are believed to have been influenced by Mogollon peoples. From these models it has been surmised that Mogollon villages were self-governing, under the leadership of civil and religious elders democratically selected. Differences of class seemed to have been at a minimum. The society was structured into clans, or groups of families with the same ancestors, the lines following the mother's side.

Food was prepared in the Mogollon home over a fire pit inside the semi-underground dwelling or in an earth oven outside the house. Special fire sticks were required to produce the necessary spark. The fire stick had several holes, in which a second rounded stick was twirled rapidly. The friction created by the stick produced enough heat to set a powder glowing. This powder was then caught in a tinder of wood chips or grass and coaxed into flames. Sometimes stones heated in the fire were dropped into a very tightly woven basket filled with water, to make it boil for cooking.

To prepare grain and other vegetable foods for cooking, the Mogollon used a variety of grinding tools made of stone. They consisted of manos, metates, mortars, and pestles. The earliest form of the metate, a simple uneven stone basin, was probably taken over from the earlier inhabitants, the gardening Cochise. Also inherited from the Cochise was a stone maul, with a full or nearly full groove in which a handle or haft could be bound with sinews.

Mogollon people learned to grind and polish small stone slabs to make useful articles, such as paint palettes, dishes, and stone smoking pipes. They also made pipes of fired clay for the ceremonial smoking of tobacco, which was first grown in America before it became known to Europeans.

One of the most important uses of stone was for spear points and, later, arrowheads, which came into general use among the Mogollon around A.D. 700–900. To a trained archaeologist the type of flint or stone used, the way in which the point is chipped, fluted, or flaked, the final shape of the projectile point, and its weight and size reveal the story of the ancient maker.

For thousands of years before the bow and arrow came into use the ancient Indians of America had employed a rude throwing stick, called the atlatl. The weapon is also called a spear-thrower. At the base of the throwing stick was a pair of loops, made of animal hide. The projectile was a spear shaft which had a sharp head fastened to its forward end. The hunter inserted his thumb and forefinger through the hide loops to hold steady the spear shaft. When the thrower brought his arm forward with a strong, overhead swing, the spear was launched. The atlatl, in effect an extension of the hunter's arm, could drive a shaft head into a target at a distance of two hundred to three hundred feet. Archaeologists have found stone spear points, which they believe had been used in atlatls as long as ten thousand years ago, by Folsom man.

The bow and arrow replaced the atlatl as the Indian's chief weapon because it had many advantages over the older spear-thrower. The bow and arrow was a more accurate weapon, even at longer range. It was easier to carry than a throwing stick, a

ATLATL

spear, or dart. The arrows for the bow were smaller and lighter versions of the atlatl dart, measuring a little more than two feet in length, just about the distance that a hunter could pull his bowstring.

In addition to meat, hunting provided the Indians with animal hides, which they used for clothing, footwear, and even material to make portable shelters. Besides the bow and arrow, snares and traps were used by Indian hunters, especially for small game or birds.

SLIP LOOP SNARE FOR CATCHING BIRDS, MIMBRES BOWL DECORATION

DEER HUNTERS WITH BOWS AND ARROWS, MIMBRES BOWL DECORATION

MAN WITH BOW AND QUIVER:
WALL PAINTING

WARRIOR WEARING ARMOR WITH QUIVER
OF ARROWS AND SHIELD, MIMBRES BOWL
DECORATION

Some of the weapons used by the ancient Indians, as well as the clothing that they wore, have been revealed as illustrations on old pieces of pottery. The early Indians developed a body armor made of cured animal hides, and they used shields made of leather.

The Mogollon Indians were the first people to make pottery in the Southwest. They used native clays. The development of pottery implies a fairly stationary home life because earthenware is too heavy and too easily broken to be carried about by people who are always on the move. Pottery changed cooking methods because it could be used over an open fire, an improvement over the old way of dropping heated stones into a perishable container filled with water.

The local clays that Mogollon potters used to make pitchers and bowls were rich in iron, which made the vessels turn a brownish color when they were put in firing ovens. The first Mogollon pottery was simple brown or reddish ware, undecorated, and useful for cooking and food storage. But with increasing skill, the pottery makers began to add decorations. The simple brown ware became highly polished. On some pots, the Indians applied a slip, a thin coating of liquid clay which turned red when the vessel was fired. Geometric designs were added by various techniques, such as brushing, incising, or scoring. This pottery type became known as red-on-white.

Indians in America did not use the potter's wheel until it was introduced by the Spaniards. Mogollon pottery was made by coiling and scraping. Ropes of clay were rolled by hand and built up, layer upon layer, to form the sides and neck of a vessel. The body walls were scraped smooth by a stone or shell. The coils can sometimes still be clearly seen in the neck areas of a pottery jug.

About the time that the bow and arrow was replacing the atlatl and the hand-thrown dart as the principal weapon of the Mogollon, several other important articles were introduced. Perhaps most significant were blankets made of fur and feathers, and cotton, which could be used to make clothing.

Around A.D. 1000, toward the end of the period of Mogollon farming in the Southwest, a distinctive kind of pottery was produced in the valley of the Mimbres River in southern New Mexico. Some of it was decorated with complex arrangements of triangles, scrolls, and zigzagging lines. The most distinctive features of Mimbres pottery are the lifelike decorations, usually painted inside bowls. Lively animal forms represent rabbits, frogs, birds, deer, and sheep. Insects are a favorite theme. Human forms are also frequent as decorations. The pictures are animated and full of spirit and movement.

MIMBRES BOWL DECORATED WITH CEREMONIAL SCENE OF MAN IN FISH COSTUME

Archaeologists have found these Mimbres bowls buried by the thousands alongside the skeletons of their owners. The ancient Mogollon of the Mimbres area believed that the bowls had magic powers and that the vessels were inhabited by the spirits of the men who made and owned them. Before the pots were buried, a

MIMBRES BOWL DECORATED WITH HORNED TOAD

GRASSHOPPER, MIMBRES BOWL DECORATION

MIMBRES BOWL DECORATED WITH KACHINA (?)

MIMBRES BOWL WITH "KILL HOLE" DECORATED WITH HUNTING SCENE

hole was punched into the base of the bowl to let the spirit of the vessel escape. The breaks are called "kill holes."

With their new farming skills, which assured the Mogollon of a full food supply, and their pottery vessels, which made it possible to cook and store the new plant foods, the people began to find themselves with unfamiliar leisure time. With their new leisure, they started to beautify their homes and villages and to decorate themselves. Art began to enrich the lives of the Mogollon people.

Now there was also time for trade to develop with neighboring people. New tools, utensils, and ornaments were introduced to the Mogollon, many of which had been brought along the mountaintops and through the river valleys, following the old routes by which the corn, beans, and squash had been carried centuries before. From the shores of the Pacific Ocean to the west came sea shells, which could be used as scraping tools or transformed into personal ornaments, such as beads, bracelets, and pendants.

For fifteen hundred years the Mogollon people lived in the valleys and along the mountainsides in the Southwest. Sometimes the soil in their cornfields became worn out and lost its fertility and a new field had to be found. At times, different homesites probably became necessary. No one really knows what happened to these Indian people, but the basic Mogollon people probably never strayed very far from the homes of their fathers. Years later, when another group of Indians left the northern plateaus and came down into the southern regions, they probably just merged into existing Mogollon communities. Indian settlements still thrive in the Rio Grande Valley.

THE HOHOKAM

MEN OF THE DESERT

About 100 B.C. or soon thereafter, when the Mogollon farmers were becoming established in the mountain and valley country of the Southwest, a related desert people also prepared to give up hunting and gathering to become agriculturalists. These Indians, perhaps another branch of the ancient Cochise, settled in the arid, hot valleys of the lower Gila and Salt rivers, which, fed by the rains running off the Colorado watershed, slake the thirst of a parched land.

The ancient Indians who made their homes along the lower Gila and Salt are known as the Hohokam, a word in the language of the modern Pima Indians that means "those who have gone before." The Hohokam became experts at using the river waters to irrigate their farming fields.

Many of the customs of the ancient Hohokam have been preserved in modern times among the Pima and Papago Indians, who are believed to be descendants of the old desert farmers. Pima Indian agriculture still employs ancient irrigation techniques. Similar styles have persisted in the houses being built and in the pottery, which is still being made.

Among the Pima Indians on their reservation in southern Arizona along the lower Gila there is a wide, dusty expanse of empty desert. The open space lies in the afternoon shadows of the Sierra Estrella, off to the west. The land is covered with mounds and hillocks, sloping off in every direction. Snakes slither along the warm sand between the rocks, feeding on the rats that burrow in the refuse piles. Called the Place of Snakes by the Pima Indians, the area is generally known as Snaketown.

EXCAVATION AT SNAKETOWN, MOUND ⚒16

The howl of the coyote can still be heard in the dusty undergrowth. Deer, cottontail rabbits, gray fox, muskrats, and water birds come down to drink the river water and to rest on the warm, sunny banks.

The Hohokam lived in Snaketown for twelve centuries. During this time they built a total of more than five thousand houses, at a rate of four hundred a year. Hohokam houses were built differently from the Mogollon pithouse structures in the eastern mountains. The Hohokam built houselike edifices inside shallow pits, which were dug in the ground, but the walls of the house structure were independent of the sides of the excavation.

Some Hohokam buildings seem to have been unusually large, perhaps square-shaped, with walls built of upright poles or sticks, chinked with mud, a method of house building called jacal construction. These houses could have been the dwellings of several families or even a community building for ceremonial purposes. Jacal-type building continued among the Hohokam for centuries, during which time the shape of the houses changed from square to oblong to oval. Some building took place on the surface of the ground, but most continued with floor levels excavated below the level of the surrounding earth.

Just inside the entrance passages to the houses were the fire pits, used for cooking and warmth.

The Hohokam village at Snaketown expanded year after year without any apparent plan. The site did not seem suitable even for defense.

Over the centuries most of the houses in Snaketown have crumbled into ruins, and they became buried under the reddish soil. The village was finally abandoned by the Hohokam around A.D. 1400.

When modern archaeologists began digging into the desert mounds and clearing away the blowing sand, they uncovered many of the buried houses. They discovered how little change there was in architectural styles in the village in the twelve hundred years from the earliest period to the latest.

Improved varieties of corn and plant foods such as squash and beans were already being planted in the desert valleys, wherever a bit of soil proved suitable and sufficient water could be supplied. But before farming could really be begun, intensive irrigation was necessary. The Pioneer Hohokam farmers became expert irrigators. At first they waited for the rivers to flood, then used the overflowing waters to refresh their growing crops. Then they dug ditches and canals, using only stone and wooden tools, to lead the water from the rivers to the planted fields. These irrigation works were the lifelines of the Hohokam, who could never have established a settled village life in the desert without them. The canals were dug by thousands of men working together for endless hours. One ditch traced at Snaketown led to a point on the Gila River, where it received its water flow, some ten miles away. Other Hohokam irrigation canals in the region are known to be even longer.

The flow of the water through the irrigation system was controlled by a series of mats, made of woven fiber, which were used to dam up the main canal. By maneuvering the mats, picking up some, setting others in place, the Hohokam farmers could divert the water into side canals, which led to the thirsty fields.

Even expert irrigation farmers, like the Hohokam, experienced their difficulties. Modern archaeologists, excavating the ancient canal systems, came across telltale evidence of a disaster that must have occurred around A.D. 900. One of the head gates of the main canal appeared to have burst, probably under the intense pressure of cascading water swollen by sudden downpours of rain. But the prehistoric, hand-dug canals were generally constructed solidly. Modern farmers, thousands of years after the canals were first put to use, still rely on them to irrigate their crops.

The Pioneer phase of the Hohokam in the river valleys of the lower Gila and the Salt rivers lasted for six centuries, ending around A.D. 500. During that time the interchange of ideas and artifacts with Mexico continued. The bow and arrow came up from the south and replaced the throwing stick, the atlatl. Cotton was introduced, both the fiber and the woven cloth.

About the same time, A.D. 500, another idea from Mexico, the ball court, reached the Hohokam in Snaketown. Ball courts in the Southwest were then built, usually oval in shape and measuring as long as two hundred feet. Games played in the courts were ceremonial, stemming from the religious life of the people.

A rubber ball, probably made from guayule, a desert bush, was found in a preserved state on a Hohokam site. The ball suggested that the ceremonial game that was played was similar to the games of the Middle Americans of Mexico.

A Hohokam ball game took on the aspects of a bloody battle between the opposing sides.

Later, another architectural idea was adopted by the Hohokam involving the building of platform mounds like the bases of the temple pyramids in Mexico. The mounds were made of earth and adobe, bricks made of mud mixed with straw and dried in the sun. Sometimes the mounds were built in successive stages. Very few traces have been found of any superstructures built on the main platform or any of its levels. The mound was probably also ceremonial in nature, to be used as a platform for dancers, musicians, pipers, and drummers.

COPPER BELLS

At one site, Gatlin, near Gila Bend, Arizona, excavations of a platform mound disclosed copper bells of the "tinkler" type, which may have been worn by ceremonial dancers. The bells seemed to have come from western and northwestern Mexico. They had been made by the "lost wax" method of copper casting, in which wax, shaped into the desired form over an inner core, is enclosed by an outer mold of clay. When heated, the melted wax is drawn off, leaving an empty space into which molten metal is poured.

Also from Mexico the Hohokam obtained mirrors, made of crystals of iron pyrites fixed on a flat plate of stone, as well as finely worked mosaic plaques, stone beads, earplugs, nose buttons, and a variety of shell ornaments.

The earliest pottery developed by the Hohokam farmers was plain red and plain buff. Later, a red-on-buff style appeared. Originally Hohokam pottery was thin-walled, built up by damp coils of clay and patted into shape with a flat paddle. This method of pottery making is called the paddle-and-anvil technique. Pottery made this way is smoothed by a wooden paddle tapped gently against a stone or other hard object held inside the vessel's walls. At first the pottery vessels were decorated with geometric designs or with small stylized elements of people or animals. Later, Hohokam pottery shapes took varied forms, often of humans, animals, birds, or reptiles.

Broken pieces of pottery, called potsherds, or shards, are like a calendar to an archaeologist. The thickness, shape, color, and decoration of the shard are clues to the period when the pottery was made. The changes in pottery styles reflect changes in the lives of the people who created them. Tens of thousands of pottery shards were selected for study from the million and a half that were unearthed at Snaketown. The changing fragments revealed the lives of the Hohokam over a period of twelve hundred years.

The earliest Hohokam made crude figurines of pottery, most of them representing the female form. The primitive effigy figures resemble pottery models made in Mexico nearby. In later phases of their culture, the Hohokam became the first Indians in America to shape pottery jars in more realistic human form.

Baked clay was also used to fashion animal forms. Sometimes the figures were three-dimensional sculptures, like the mountain sheep that was found in a grave. The vessel was used to burn incense on religious or ceremonial occasions.

A favorite design motif on Hohokam pottery was the snake. Snake forms were also used to decorate shells and incense burners made of stone. The snake is often shown being attacked by a bird.

Stone was an essential material, used both for tools and weapons and for decoration and ornament. Stone manos and metates were skillfully fashioned to grind corn and seeds, and mortars

POTTERY ANIMAL FIGURES FROM SNAKETOWN

and pestles to pulverize nuts and berries. Hohokam stoneworkers made polished stone axes, scrapers, knives, bowls, incense burners, and flat trays, or palettes, which were used to hold pigments and mix body and face paint. The desert people painted themselves for religious games and ceremonies.

Grinding trays for cosmetics were derived from the earlier corn-grinding mano and metate. These palettes were often carved in the shape of a desert creature, a horned toad, a lizard, a snake, or a bird. A horned toad, carved of stone, with a flat trough for grinding cosmetics, was found in Snaketown. It was smashed into countless bits but has been restored.

The stone projectile points made by the Hohokam Indians provided evidence of the diminishing importance of hunting to a farming people. At first the projectile types were large and heavy dart points. Later, the spearheads gave way to long, very slender points, barbed and stemmed, which were designed as arrow tips. Even later, Hohokam projectile types became small, finely

STONE PALETTE FROM SNAKETOWN

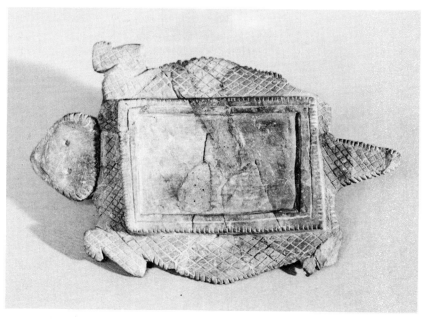

chipped triangular heads, with side notches, similar to the types used by Anasazi neighbors to the north.

Desert rock was also used to make animal figures, usually in the form of dogs, lizards, or toads, to be used as incense burners. Once in a while a human figure was made. The stone vessels and figurines were probably used for magical or religious reasons.

Trading developed not only with the Indians of Mexico but also with the people of California, from whom the Hohokam acquired sea shells for decoration and personal ornament. Shells had many additional uses as scraping tools.

The first Hohokam Pioneers proved to be energetic people. Around A.D. 500 they began to spread out from the desert valleys, moving up along the rivers and establishing new settlements near the Verde River in the north and the upper Gila and Santa Cruz rivers to the northeast. For four centuries this colonizing impulse continued. Wherever the Hohokam moved, they carried with them the influence of their customs and accomplishments, includ-

HOHOKAM STONE BOWL

STONE VESSEL FROM SNAKETOWN

ing the urge to build ball courts for sacred games. As a result these ceremonial areas have been found in many places throughout the Southwest.

For the succeeding three hundred years, A.D. 900–1200, the Hohokam stayed in the areas that they had colonized, developing their skills and improving their crafts. The period was quiet and sedentary. During this calm time the Hohokam perfected a method of etching designs on the surface of shells, using an acid solution made from the fruit of the saguaro, the giant cactus plant. The process of etching was developed by the Indians three centuries before the technique was used by armor makers in medieval Europe—who are often believed to have originated it.

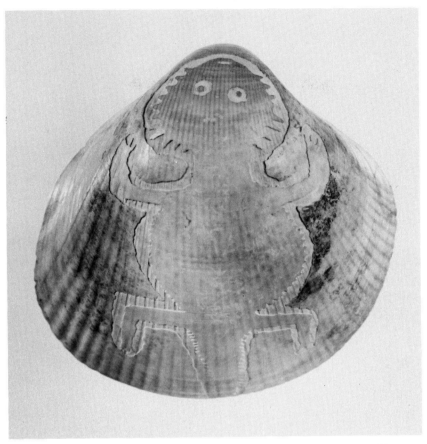

ETCHED CLAM SHELL WITH FIGURE OF TOAD, FROM SNAKETOWN

A well-known example of etching by the Hohokam process is a shell with the figure of a horned toad.

To make his etching, the Hohokam artist covered the surface of the shell with pitch or wax, in which he scratched a design. He then soaked the shell in a weak acid solution, which he prepared from the fermented juice of the saguaro fruit. The acid ate away the surface of the shell wherever it was not coated by the protecting pitch or wax. When the pitch was removed, the unaffected areas revealed the artist's design.

Shell could be shaped into many forms for ornaments. Animals, fish, and birds were popular.

Around A.D. 1200 the Hohokam seemed to have reached the

HOHOKAM SHELL PENDANTS

peak of their expansion, and a period of retreat and decline set in. The next two centuries are called a classic period, but the Hohokam, feeling themselves pushed by new peoples coming from the north, began to pull back. Settlements by earlier Hohokam in the northern river valleys were abandoned, and the people turned back to their original territories in the desert.

But the Hohokam began to leave even their homelands in the southern Arizona desert around A.D. 1400 and journey to destinations still unknown. Some, however, probably remained in the desert, where they became the forebears of the Pima and Papago Indians, who were there when the first Spanish explorers arrived late in the seventeenth century.

THE SINAGUA, SALADO, AND COHONINA

THE PEOPLE IN BETWEEN

The San Francisco Peaks loom against the sky in northern Arizona, surrounded by a volcanic field that covers some three thousand square miles. The area is filled with rocky peaks, cinder cones, and lava flows formed by volcanic activity which occurred over a time span of several million years. Sometimes the eruptions were violent; other times the molten lava poured out of the earth quietly.

According to ancient Indian belief, the San Francisco Peaks was the home of the kachina spirits. Long ago the kachinas quarreled with the people of earth and refused to come down from the mountain heights to lend a helping hand where it was needed. Instead, the Hopi, Zuñi, and other Indian people don masks and impersonate the kachinas in ceremonial dances.

Around A.D. 600 some Indian farming bands moved into the area near the peaks and set up pithouses in shallow excavations dug in the earth, near the volcanic fields. The ancient dwellings were ideal for the climate, keeping out the summer heat and the winter cold. Because there are few springs or wells in the area, the Indians learned to farm the land near the edges of the ancient cinder fields, which managed to retain whatever moisture was available. The technique is known as dry farming.

The Indians had been living peacefully near the mountains for over 450 years when suddenly, in A.D. 1065, the earth roared and trembled in a violent volcanic eruption. Fiery globs of molten lava were blown out of the depths of the earth, and a mound of smoking black rocks and ashes piled up higher and higher.

SAN FRANCISCO PEAKS

The people were terrified and fled from their homes, as the sky grew dark with clouds of ash and as cinders rained onto their fields. The upheaval of the earth created a symmetrical cone of volcanic cinders one thousand feet high, now known as Sunset Crater. Streams of black lava flowed at its base, and a cloud of black ash floated down from the sky and blanketed eight hundred square miles of the surrounding earth.

When the volcano subsided, the Indians moved back, uncertainly at first, then eagerly. The ash had covered the earth with a porous layer which formed a mulch, trapping the moisture and reducing the amount of water that evaporated from the surface. The cinders over the fields formed into a mineral-rich soil, ideal for agriculture. The catastrophe had been transformed into a blessing.

The Indians' skill at farming these fields prompted modern archaeologists to give them the name Sinagua, a word derived from the Spanish phrase meaning "without water."

Word of the new, fertile fields spread to friends and relatives nearby, who promptly moved into the area. The rich soil attracted other Southwestern people, some from the dry desert lands in the south, others from the mountains and plateau country, some even from the valleys farther west. The meeting of the different peoples from various sections resulted in an interchange of customs and skills. The people from the high plateau country were excellent house builders, with new techniques for using sun-dried adobe and stone. The Hohokam from southern Arizona could share their skills at digging canals and irrigation ditches. The Mogollon, who came from the south and east, may have inspired the red-on-brown pottery, which came to be made in the area. However, the Sinagua potters used a different method of pottery making, which probably came from the west: the paddle-and-anvil technique, used by the Hohokam, Cohonina, and the Indians of the lower Colorado River Valley. Pottery made by the paddle-and-anvil method has coils of clay, not scraped smooth, but patted into shape with a wooden paddle and a stone or other hard object held against the inside of the vessel's walls.

Soon, villages were established near Sunset Crater, reflecting the new ways of building. One was Wupatki, which was inhabited for centuries. "Wupatki" is a word of the Hopi Indians, which means "tall house," indicating the change from the semi-underground pithouses built by the original Sinagua settlers. Wupatki was situated near one of the few springs in the area. During the twelfth century, the structures at Wupatki contained over one hundred rooms and reached heights of three stories. The mingling of Indian cultures was also evidenced in the building of an open-air amphitheater, a unique unroofed structure resembling a ceremonial Anasazi kiva, and a ball court, made of stone masonry.

The volcanic fields were productive for almost 150 years, but continuous farming drained the soil. The very winds that had

RUINS AT WUPATKI

carried the magic ash kept blowing and stripped away the cover of cinders. Early in the thirteenth century a drought set in, and the people were forced to abandon the area, never to return.

The severe dry spell drove many of the residents of Sunset Crater into the nearby valley of the Verde River, where dry farming was not possible. The people were forced to concentrate near existing irrigation ditches, fed by permanent springs. Already in the Verde Valley were groups of the Sinagua who had entered the area a century earlier. When the Sinagua had first arrived, they found the valley the home of a peaceful people living quietly in simple huts made of branches and brush near patches of corn, beans, pumpkins, and cotton. The Sinagua, with advanced construction skills, built houses of masonry along the cliffsides and on the high mesas. The first settlement, which had been built around A.D. 1125, was a small cluster of fifteen or twenty rooms at Tuzigoot on a shelf of land 120 feet above the river valley. The building originally could accommodate about fifty persons.

As the Great Drought that gripped the Southwest during the thirteenth century forced the Indians off their fields, the population at Tuzigoot doubled and redoubled. By the end of the century there were ninety-two rooms on the hilltop overlooking the Verde River. Around Tuzigoot six other settlements were established by farmers fleeing their parched fields.

On a cliffside along the Verde River, not far from Tuzigoot, the Sinagua built a house, which has been mistakenly named Montezuma's Castle. Montezuma was the most famous emperor of the Aztecs of Mexico. The mistake was made by modern settlers who

BALL COURT AT WUPATKI

RUINS AT TUZIGOOT, VERDE RIVER IN FOREGROUND

thought that no one but the Aztecs could have built so imposing a structure.

Near the cliff dwelling is a great natural well, also named after Montezuma. Countless gallons of water flow from the well every day to irrigate the fields nearby. The well was also regarded as a religious site.

In addition to the Sinagua and the Cohonina, signs in the Southwest point to another Indian people, who have been named the Salado. They used stone tools and made a distinctive type of pottery: brown with decorations in red and black.

The relationship of the Salado Indians with the mountain Mogollon and the desert Hohokam is not yet clear. At some time in the past the Salado probably spilled peacefully out of the eastern mountains and moved into village sites in the low desert lands. Some of the villages had apparently been abandoned, while others were probably still occupied. The Salado seemed to

MONTEZUMA'S CASTLE

have lived peacefully side by side with the Hohokam for more than a century. Near what is now Phoenix, Arizona, they erected a structure with walls more than a meter thick, enclosing a dozen or so rooms. The building has been named Casa Grande (Spanish for Great House). For many years Casa Grande, despite the usual desert atmosphere, kept crumbling under the onslaught of sun and rain. In recent years a protecting roof has been set over the structure in an effort to preserve it.

The thick walls of Casa Grande were probably erected to provide a defense against enemy marauders. These raiders might

CASA GRANDE, SALADO RUIN

SALADO POLYCHROME POT

have been an offshoot of the Hohokam, who had never accepted a peaceful way of life with their neighbors, or they may have been the late-comers, the Athapascan-speaking Apache.

Whoever the enemy was, the Salado, with the Hohokam, abandoned the valleys of the Gila and Salt rivers sometime after A.D. 1400 and either went north to join the Anasazi or turned east to merge with groups of the Mogollon.

THE PATAYAN

A distinctive group of southwestern Indians appeared around A.D. 600 near the lower drainage of the Colorado River. They occupied an area that extended from the delta of the river to the northern territory of the Cohonina Indians and stretched eastward for some distance into Arizona. These Indians are known as the Patayan, a name that means "old people" or "ancient ones" in the language of the modern Yumas.

Sometimes another name is used to describe these ancient Indians: Hakataya, the Yuman name for the Colorado River.

The Patayan were a Yuman-speaking people who farmed the fields left fertile by the seasonal flooding of the lower Colorado River. During times of flood the Patayan scattered in small groups into the surrounding mountains and desert to hunt for game and to forage for edible plants. When the waters receded, they returned to their fields to cultivate their crops.

Over a period of centuries the flooding waters of the Colorado River drowned many Patayan sites and buried them under layers of silt and debris. Nevertheless, archaeologists have found evidence of Patayan life, which was significantly different from that of their neighbors. Using the paddle-and-anvil method, the Patayan made a simple gray-brown ware, which was occasionally decorated with red paint. The metate used to grind corn was generally trough-shaped. Their houses were jacal-walled—tree trunks set in the ground and lashed together. The people knew about digging canals to irrigate their fields, but they seemed to prefer the natural floodwaters of the river.

Pottery appeared among the Patayan around A.D. 600, according to some estimates. Pots, which were molded in baskets, had notched rims. Large water jars had a sharp-angled hump called a

Colorado shoulder. This early Patayan period lasted for about five hundred years. On later Patayan pottery the shoulder disappeared, and the burnished red ware was replaced by round bowls, large trays, and stucco-finished pottery often with red-on-buff painting. The grinding stones became more rectangular in shape. Shell for personal jewelry was brought in from the Pacific Ocean and the Gulf of California. During this time the Patayan expanded, leaving the Mojave Basin to spread east into Arizona and west and south into southern California and Mexico.

Around A.D. 1500 the Patayan culture took on its distinct Yuman character.

The Patayan were probably descended from the ancient hunters and gatherers of the Mojave Desert region of the Great Basin, in all probability one of the ancient branches of the Cochise.

The Patayan themselves are considered to be the ancestors of the modern Yuman-speaking Indians, the Yumas, the Cocopah, the Maricopa, the Havasupai, the Mojave, and the Walapai, who live in the valleys of the lower Colorado and Gila rivers.

MODERN POTTERY DOLLS, MADE BY MOJAVE INDIANS, DESCENDANTS OF THE PATAYAN

ANASAZI: BASKETMAKERS
AND PUEBLOS

High tablelands, some of them a mile and a half above sea level, make up the Southwestern or Colorado Plateau, which includes the Four Corners area, where the states of New Mexico, Arizona, Utah, and Colorado touch. The flat plateaus are called mesas, a Spanish word meaning "table" or "tableland."

The high mesa country abounds with dramatic rock formations, colorful buttes, and domed mountains. Fields of lava flow are dominated by volcanic cones, some rising more than eleven thousand feet. Mountainsides are covered with forest stands of pine and juniper. The flat table tops sustain patches of grass and sagebrush. The mesas stretch off to the horizon for miles, cut by deep gorges in which rivers wander through valleys between sheer canyon walls.

The San Juan River flows westward through the heart of the mesa country, skirting close by the Four Corners area and emptying into the Colorado. Southward the tablelands extend toward the Mogollon Rim and include the valley of the Little Colorado River, which joins the Colorado just above the Grand Canyon. The eastern end of the mesas extends beyond the region of the northern Rio Grande and includes the valley of the Pecos River. On the Pacific side of the Continental Divide the plateau country stretches over the Colorado River and into Nevada.

Vegetation on the mesas was not ideal for deer, bears, or mountain sheep, but there was forage for smaller animals. The rivers and water holes attracted flocks of fowl, which could be caught, and there were supplies of wild roots and edible berries, which were adequate to sustain life. The earliest people on the mesas were akin to the hunting and gathering Cochise, who had started from the Great Basin centuries earlier. Through them the earliest Indians of the plateau country were linked to all other people of the Southwest.

The climate on the plateaus is dry and cool, with sparse and erratic rainfall. But there was enough good soil along the rivers and an adequate climate to permit corn to be planted and to ripen. The growing season was long enough for the needs of early gardeners with their patches of primitive corn and squash, obtained from neighboring tribesmen to the south.

Archaeologists have dug up relics of early plateau dwellers in the form of intricate baskets. The people were therefore given the name Basketmakers to distinguish them from the later pottery makers. Pottery remains were found only in layers of earth on top of the early burials in which baskets were found. The baskets that the archaeologists discovered were made with considerable skill, but they believe that there must have been a prior period when a more simple type of basket was in use, even though no such basket has yet been found. If such traces are found, they will probably be dated before the first century B.C.

The more intricate baskets that were found in cave shelters and graves showed that the Indians had become experts at using plant fibers to make baskets. The baskets found were of yucca, straw, vines, rushes, and even twigs. The first baskets of this period, known as Early Basketmaker, which spanned five hundred years, from about 100 B.C. to A.D. 400, were made of plant fibers loosely plaited, coiled, or stitched. The finished baskets were decorated with simple designs in black or red or both. Later, the decoration of baskets became very elaborate.

Along with the baskets, found in the graves were the skeletal remains of ancient people, who had been buried dressed in string aprons and loincloths, made of animal hair, furs, and feathers. The graves also yielded bags made of cedar or juniper bark, sandals woven of reed or yucca fibers, stone tools, and spearheads, as well as objects of bone and wood. But in the grave levels that were examined, no clay vessels, nor any early forms of baked or fired pottery, were found.

Several of the earliest Basketmaker sites, located in the north-

BASKETMAKER CARRYING BASKET

ern San Juan region, near Durango, Colorado, were occupied for
three hundred years, from A.D. 46 to A.D. 330. One site is known
as Talus Slope Village and is located on a high bank over the
Animas River, not far from its confluence with the San Juan.
Nearby is the farthest northern reach of the Colorado Plateau,
and beyond are the Rocky Mountains. The area is filled with wild
animal life—deer, mountain sheep, squirrels and other animals.

Rock shelter caves near the Talus Slope Village have preserved
deposits of maize, squash, and wild food plants, like amaranth,
sunflower seeds, and mustard. The Basketmaker Indians continued hunting and collecting wild plants, while at the same time
cultivating corn and pumpkins. The corn found in the Durango
sites proved to be more advanced than the earliest Mogollon

maize from Bat Cave. Its type is known as Hohokam-Basket-maker maize.

Found in graves at the Durango site were baskets, bark bags and weapons, tools, and varied ceremonial objects. Also found were some fragments that may have been unfired clay containers or figurines. But no baked-clay vessels could be found in any of the digs.

Four hundred years passed before the Basketmakers learned to make fired earthenware. Around A.D. 400 the Basketmakers had become experts at making pottery, an art that they probably adopted from the Mogollon Indians to the south of them. In spite

CRADLE BOARD

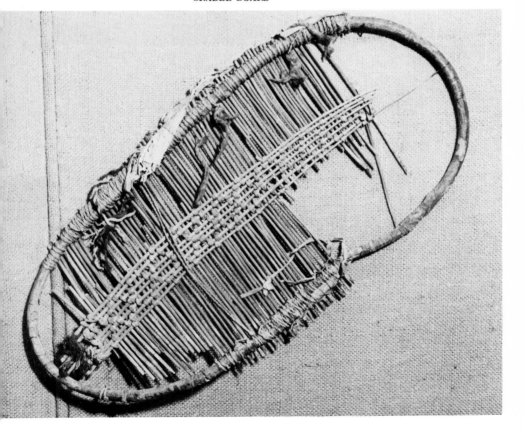

of the fact that they were now making pottery, the people of the mesas, who lived during the three centuries from A.D. 400 to 700, are still referred to as the Basketmakers.

About the same time that pottery was coming into use among the mesa dwellers, other far-reaching changes were taking place in the high country. Beans were introduced, to be planted between the corn stalks. The wild turkey was domesticated, although at first for its feathers rather than its meat. An improved grinding tool was the open-ended metate, which replaced the earlier types. The Indians learned to use a polished ax, grooved where it was bound to the handle. And of greatest importance, they began to make cotton cloth and to use the bow and arrow, which replaced the atlatl. The three centuries A.D. 400 to 700 are called by archaeologists Modified or Late Basketmaker.

But the descendants of the Basketmakers, who lived on the mesas after the dawn of the eighth century, are known by a new name. By that time they had become skillful builders, capable of constructing complex stone structures. These Indians have come to be known as Pueblos, a name derived from the Spanish word for village.

The Basketmakers and the prehistoric Pueblos are all grouped together under one name, Anasazi—a Navajo Indian word, which means "ancient ones" or "ancient enemies."

The new tools and the new plant foods inspired the Pueblos to improve their farming techniques. Water was vital, but the rainfall could not be relied upon to provide for the growing crops. The uncontrolled rainfalls could, in addition, accumulate and burst forth suddenly in flash floods, which came roaring down the canyons, wiping out whole fields in their paths.

And as the Pueblo people crowded together in small village communities, water reserves became even more essential.

The water problem was solved by the Indians by terracing their fields in "steps" and by building check dams to control the flow of the rains. Diversion channels were then dug to regulate irrigation for the fields. One ancient waterway, used centuries ago in southwestern Colorado, was four miles long.

The skill of the Basketmakers at handling natural fibers and vines passed on to the Pueblos, who proved to be very adept at making sandals and footwear, as well as baskets. Over hundreds of years fashions in Indian footgear changed. At first sandals were woven with square toes and adorned with fringes of twined cord. Later the styles changed to scalloped toes with color designs on the upper side and woven patterns on the lower. Another shift in fashion was to a round toe, and an even later development was the notched toe.

Changes also took place in the style of clothing worn by the Anasazi. Early materials consisted of strips of fur and turkey feathers, woven on a cord of yucca fiber. But when cotton became available by trade with southern neighbors, it served for clothing and subsequently blankets. Cotton was imported in the form of both yarn and cloth. It could not be grown in the mountain highlands because the growing season was not long enough for the plant to ripen.

Through trade, the mesa dwellers had also become familiar with shell, which could be used for ornaments. Abalone shell came from the Pacific Coast, and about the same time turquoise began to be used for ornament and decoration. Salt was another article that was added to the growing trade.

Before the Anasazi learned to make true, fired pottery around A.D. 400, the Basketmakers had carried water and other liquids in animal skins or in baskets covered with pitch. They also used clay that had not been fired to line baskets. A clay liner prevented a basket from burning when corn or seeds were shaken with live coals and parched.

But the Basketmakers quickly mastered the art of pottery making, especially the ring-coil method, in which circles of clay were set on top of one another to build up the walls of the vessel. The indentations between the coils were smoothed away and the vessel baked in an outdoor oven. The firing turned the pot gray or gray-white. The earliest decorations were usually on the inside of open bowls and consisted of squares, triangles, or other geometric shapes—zigzagging, parallel, stepped, or waving lines, triangles, frets, and checkers. The designs seemed to have a resemblance to the decorations painted in coiled baskets by the preceding Basketmakers.

Around A.D. 700 a form of pottery was made for household use by a technique in which the coiled strips of clay in the neck of the cooking jars were not smoothed away. The method was

NECK-BANDED POTTERY JAR

known as "neck banding." The simple pottery forms of the Basket-makers gave way to a series of curious new shapes, and vessels made like birds or ducks, bottles with triple-lobed bodies, ring bodies, and stirrup mouths now appeared on the mesas. No one is sure where the idea for these strange shapes originated. Possibly, the pottery forms were first created on the mesas. The new phase of pottery making lasted for two centuries, A.D. 700 to 900, the period known as Pueblo I.

Around 900 a new technique of pottery making came into use, marking the beginning of Pueblo II. The ring-coil method gave way to spiral coiling, in which a rope of clay is formed and

BOTTLE, PUEBLO II

PITCHER, PUEBLO II

POTTERY BOWL AND LADLE, PUEBLO II

CANTEEN, PUEBLO II

PITCHER, PUEBLO II

POTTERY VESSEL WITH STIRRUP SPOUT, EARLY PUEBLO III

JAR, EARLY PUEBLO III

LADLE, EARLY PUEBLO III

wound continuously in a more or less unbroken strand, building up the body walls of the pottery vessel.

The period of Pueblo II lasted for the two centuries 900 to 1100. During this period a corrugated earthenware became popular as a cooking dish. Pottery decoration remained strongly black-on-white, sometimes in the form of broad lines and bold shapes, but usually geometric, like the earlier practice.

During the next two hundred years, 1100 to 1300, the phase called Pueblo III, Anasazi ceramics reached a peak of excellence, with black-on-white styles produced in the eastern areas around Chaco Canyon and Mesa Verde and a western type, black-red-and-white-on-orange, made near Kayenta, Arizona. The eastern

MUG, MESA VERDE BLACK AND WHITE, PUEBLO III

group used paint rich in iron and carbon; the western potters used primarily a carbon paint. In the east the pigments were applied after the vessel had been polished, making the design patterns stand out vividly against the shiny background. The western pottery makers painted the design on the vessel walls before they were completely polished, with the result that the color and design seemed to fade into the surface.

New pottery shapes made an appearance—pitchers, mugs, ladles, open bowls, and even some effigy forms. The vessels were decorated with complicated arrangements of triangles, bands, frets, and spirals.

The last prehistoric phase of the Anasazi is called Pueblo IV. It extended from 1300 until their domination by the Spanish in the late seventeenth century. During these four centuries Pueblo pottery became increasingly colorful, culminating in the red-and-

CEREMONIAL BOWL, PUEBLO III

BOWL

black-on-yellow polychrome, still made by the modern Hopi Indians, and the black-on-tan wares of the Rio Grande region today.

As their name, Pueblo, indicates, however, the greatest achievements of the Indians were building houses and villages.

The Basketmakers lived in semi-underground houses, set in shallow saucerlike excavations, with walls of logs and mortar stacked on a foundation of tree trunks laid in horizontal rows. The walls supported the roof. Remains of Basketmaker pithouses have been found in the Talus Slope Village near Durango on the sides of a slope overlooking the Animas River. Two terraces were cut to provide a level floor for some thirty-five houses, many of them built over the ruins of previously abandoned structures.

The houses were entered by a small doorway. They were warmed by a central fire pit in which large heated stones were placed. Inside these semi-underground shelters were storage pits, for grain, dug in the floor. Some of the underground storage chambers were bottle-shaped; some were open, lined with stone, with dome-shaped or "beehive" covers made of clay and decorated. Animal tracks and claw marks were frequent design elements, punched or incised in the beehive tops.

MUG, PUEBLO III

The remains of another Modified Basketmaker settlement were found at Shabik'eshchee in the Chaco Canyon region of New Mexico. The village, occupied sometime between A.D. 400 and 700, was a small community, even for Basketmakers. It contained eighteen pit dwellings, a large kiva, and forty-eight storage bins, near an open area. Pithouses were discovered built inside the remains of earlier pithouses which seem to have been abandoned. The village was probably established, then deserted and subsequently occupied for a second time. The houses were scattered in a rough semicircle with the kiva near the center of the curve. The houses were generally oval or rectangular in shape, with the straight sides becoming more and more popular as time passed. These pit structures were lined with stone slabs, coated with mud plaster. The upper walls of the main chamber were jacal-built, formed by sticks resting on the surface of the ground outside the pit and leaning against the crossbeams of the roof. The wooden walls were covered with mud, twigs, and bark. Four posts supported a roof structure of crossbeams, covered with brush. The house was entered by a passage, usually on the southern side.

Sometimes these passages ended in a small antechamber half underground.

Inside the main room was a fire pit, which was screened against sudden drafts of cold air by an upright slab of stone, acting as a deflector or shield. In the floor near the fire basin was a circular hole, which may have been thought to be the spot where the spirit ancestors of the Indians could emerge from the underworld. In present-day ceremonial chambers, or kivas, the Pueblo still have a hole in the floor, called a sipapu, for this purpose.

The ceremonial kiva at Shabik'eshchee was a round structure built in a pit with walls faced with stone slabs. The roof, supported by four posts, had an opening through which smoke could escape. The hole served also as the entranceway into the kiva. Inside the chamber, built around the circular base of its walls, was a low bench of rock and adobe. For a long time the pithouses remained the most common form of dwelling on the mesa. Sometimes they were built in clusters of three to six structures instead of individual, isolated units. Four of these clusters would make up a village. Each village might have a building set up above the ground to serve as a storage structure, or even a dwelling unit.

The change from the semi-underground pithouse to houses above the ground is reflected in the name by which the ancient Indians are now called. The Basketmakers became known as the Pueblos, or village builders.

In one area in the Little Colorado region of eastern Arizona, the remains of early Pueblo architecture also reveal jacal structures built for storage purposes, while pithouses were still being lived in. In a second excavation in the Piedra region of Colorado the pithouses seem to have been replaced by jacal buildings all built above the ground. Most of the surface structures were single units, built closely together, but some shared walls in common. The buildings were arranged in what seems to be an arc or an irregular row. With one group of these surface buildings there was a single pithouse, which was probably a kiva.

The changes that took place in the architectural techniques of the early Pueblo Indians can be seen at Alkali Ridge in Utah in the northern region of the San Juan River. A village has been found, consisting of four aboveground dwellings, each with thirty to fifty rooms, all connected. The rooms, used both as dwelling areas and as storage spaces, were arranged in long arcs, within which were small courtyards containing two to four pithouses as ceremonial chambers. The buildings were primarily jacal-built of standing sticks plastered with mud, but small rocks were also being used as a building material, together with tree trunks serving as posts.

Pueblo architecture continued to develop new forms even while the old styles persisted, century after century. Around A.D. 900, however, a profound change seems to have come over the pattern of settlement. Large village units were dispersed, giving way to small, scattered habitations, probably the home of a single family. Here and there a solitary, multi-unit structure was built, which could have been the residence of a large family group.

During this period, Pueblo II, which lasted for the two centuries from 900 to 1100, a major change took place in the nature of the building material being used in the plateau country. Instead of poles plastered with mud, builders turned to stone masonry, which could be set in courses, row upon row. Stonework was used in the building of underground kivas, too. The wooden posts that supported the kiva roofs were superseded by pilasters of masonry.

The changes were evident in two sites at Alkali Ridge. One contained two small rectangular buildings built on the surface on foundations of posts packed with adobe and small rock. Nearby was a circular, subterranean kiva, with typical fire pit, ventilator shaft, and sipapu hole in the ground, but with four floor posts supporting the roof. A different site at Alkali Ridge revealed the building changes. In the second locality the rooms were made of stone masonry. The kiva, just south of the stone building, also had a fire pit, a ventilator, and a sipapu hole. But this kiva structure included a wall bench of stone along the base of the interior wall and six masonry pilasters rising from the bench to support the roof.

By the year 900 the pithouses had been transformed into completely underground ceremonial chambers. The kivas—a modern Hopi word—are still used by Pueblo Indians. Centuries ago, every ancient village had one or more kivas just as modern communities still do.

Indian ceremonial life in the kivas still turns toward the San

Francisco Peaks in northern Arizona, where the ancient kachinas are believed to reside. The cult of the kachina shows itself to this day in the form of small wooden figures, carved from the cottonwood tree. The kachina figures are made for children so that they may become familiar with the spirits in the mountains.

Around 1000 another change took place in the life pattern of the Pueblos. In addition to the village clusters scattered along the mesa tops, the Indians began to erect large building complexes, with structures set side by side and stories piling up on top of one another. The buildings could house many people. The era is known as the age of the Great Pueblos.

Some of these multi-unit structures were built inside caves and under the natural overhangs along the sheer canyon walls at Mesa Verde, the Canyon de Chelly, Keet Seel, and Betatakin. Others were built on the surface of open mesas in Chaco Canyon, Aztec, and Hovenweep.

Twelve towns were built in Chaco Canyon, the largest of which was Pueblo Bonito, a huge D-shaped building complex containing eight hundred rooms, set on the floor of the valley against the towering sides of the mesa. Pueblo Bonito covers

GREAT KIVA AT AZTEC, AFTER RECONSTRUCTION

GREAT KIVA AT CHACO CANYON, BEFORE RECONSTRUCTION

three acres. It is four stories high and rises in a series of terraced steps. The structure is made of stone set in rows or courses, which served as facings to cover interior cores of rock and adobe rubble. Building the complex edifice took almost 150 years. At the height of its use, it was occupied by an estimated twelve hundred persons.

The inhabitants of Pueblo Bonito probably lived in the outer rooms, which had doors and windows facing the courtyard. Rooms without exterior openings were storage areas. The open roof tops and the courtyards inside the D-shaped structure were for cooking and for food grinding and preparation.

The building at Pueblo Bonito demonstrated another change that seems to have come over Indian life in the Southwest.

WHITE HOUSE, CANYON DE CHELLY

CLIFF DWELLINGS, KEET SEEL

Nowhere in the edifice are there any doors or windows opening to the outside, beyond the compound. Any openings that may have existed at an early period had been sealed up, including a main gate on the south side. Entrance to Pueblo Bonito could be gained only by climbing a ladder over the wall.

What seem like defensive measures at Pueblo Bonito reflect a general air of uneasiness that gripped the Anasazi-Pueblo people toward the end of the eleventh century. Other large Pueblo towns were also modifying their architecture to provide additional protection: doubling the thickness of the walls of the large structures and erecting watchtowers from which an eye could be kept on all approaches to the Indian fields and settlements.

During this period many of the early Pueblo settlements sprawling in the open countryside were abandoned. The people left good farming land in the outlying regions and crowded together around the water sources. They banded together in compact villages on the tops of the mesas and built elaborate structures, rising as high as four stories. Some of the buildings contained hundreds of rooms.

There is a possibility that some wandering tribesmen, attracted by the cornfields, may have threatened the Pueblo communities. Just about this time the Athapascans were approaching the borders of the Southwest. The harvest of beans and squash stored away against the needs of the winters would have been strong magnets for hungry people. The threat of an attack and the peril of pillage can be imagined. But wandering bands were probably not much of a threat to the established Pueblo towns. Another possibility is that the Pueblos had begun quarreling among themselves.

The dwellings on the sides of the cliffs and in the overhangs along the mountainsides were also seemingly designed for defense. One cliff house, for example, could be entered only through low tunnels, just big enough to allow a person to crawl through. A crowded crawl space would have been easily defended against an invader. Other cliff houses were built at the end of difficult trails which could be easily protected.

But no signs of any conflict have been found near any of these entranceways. If a struggle had taken place on the way to the cliff houses, burn marks or other scars would certainly have disfigured the walls.

Towers, possibly for defense, were built in the Cliff Palace compound at Mesa Verde in the northern region of the San Juan River. Cliff Palace consists of a complex of buildings, containing over two hundred rooms, built of masonry inside a natural niche in the side of a sandstone wall. Under the overhang there are, in addition, twenty-three kivas, mostly round and small, each with a low circular bench and six masonry pilasters supporting the roof. Masonry at Mesa Verde consists of roughly dressed stone, unlike Chaco, where the construction had cores of rubble. Some archaeologists regard the towers at Cliff Palace not as defense posts, but as ceremonial buildings or even primitive observatories of the stars.

One certain change that was taking place was in the climate and in the conditions of the soil in the Southwest. A long period of extreme drought began, broken by occasional rain. The drought lasted from 1276 to 1293, during which time the water table throughout the area dropped and the soil generally grew drier. The change of climate was reflected in lighter snowfalls and a short winter. The frozen soil melted sooner in the year, and the melting ice drained away before the planting season was under way. The result was that the farmers who grew their crops on the mesas by dry-land farming could no longer rely on the moisture stored up by the winter freeze. The plants could not root properly in the thirsty soil.

The soil itself, farmed unceasingly for hundreds of years, was probably beginning to lose its natural fertility. At times the earth was washed away by uncontrolled cloudbursts, which poured down through the canyons in sudden flash floods, drowning everything in their paths.

The change of the winter climate and the shifting patterns of the rainfall might not have had serious consequences outside of the Southwest. But in the mountains the growing season—between planting and harvesting—is so critically short that the loss of even little time could spell disaster for the crops.

Whatever the reason, many of the Anasazi Pueblo Indians abandoned their homes in the high country during the last years of the thirteenth century and moved away, leaving almost everything behind. Some walked southwest into the valley of the Little Colorado and its tributaries, where they set about, with their building skills, constructing terraced apartment-house units of stone masonry, both block and adobe, grouped around central plazas. Their principal sites were near the Zuñi and Hopi Indian towns, which are inhabited to this day. Traveling eastward, some Pueblos reached the Pecos River almost at the edge of the plateau country, stopped, and settled down. Others moved southward into the Rio Grande and made homes in the midst of the tribesmen who had originally settled the area. The new arrivals were probably related to the original Rio Grande people through remote ancestors, even though they had come to speak different

CLIFF DWELLINGS, BETATAKIN

CLIFF PALACE, MESA VERDE

languages. The descendants of both the mesa people and the river tribes are still living today in the adobe pueblos along the Rio Grande. Their houses are the color of the earth to which they cling. The mountains loom against the sky, and the sacred waters come down from the mountains to slake the thirst of the fields.

Some names among the Rio Grande Indians no longer recall the ancient days before the Europeans put an end to the unwritten history of the ancient tribes. Now the Indian names read with echoes of the Spanish explorers who became the new masters of the land. The Indian pueblos are now called San Felipe, Santa Clara, Santo Domingo, San Ildefonso, San Juan, Laguna (meaning "lake"), and Isleta (meaning "small island"). Some names may still be links to the past, like the Zuñi or the Hopi, who are still known by a shortened version of their ancient name—"the peaceful ones." Other descendants of the ancient Indians live in pueblos named Sia, Cochiti, and Acoma. Still others are called Nambe, Tesuque, Taos, Picuris, and Jemez.

The Athapascan-speaking Indians, who came last, still occupy great areas of the Southwest. They are the Apache: the San Carlos, Tonto, and Mescalero. The Apache de Navajo, better known simply as the Navajo, still refer to themselves by their ancient name—Diné, or "people."

The links with the past endure: by the Yuman-speaking people with the Patayan, by the Pima and Papago with the Hohokam, and by the Rio Grande tribes with the Mogollon and Anasazi, all ancient Indian people of the Southwest.

INDEX

Page numbers in italics refer to illustrations and captions.

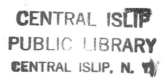

✓ 75

Bcg/89

DATE DUE Copy #1

12/75

970.4 **Tamarin, Alfred**
T   Ancient Indians of the
         Southwest   X48978

CENTRAL ISLIP PUBLIC LIBRARY

Loan Period: Two Weeks
New Books: One Week

Overdue Charges:
5¢ per day per book
Maximum Fine: $1.00/book

Archaeological Region
of the Southwe